IF EVERYONE WERE RICH, WHO WOULD MAKE ME DINNER?

If Everyone Were Rich, Who Would Make Me Dinner?

You're Not Insane—It Really Is Tough to Become Wealthy!

Joseph G. Rouse, CPA

iUniverse, Inc.
New York Lincoln Shanghai

If Everyone Were Rich, Who Would Make Me Dinner?

You're Not Insane—It Really Is Tough to Become Wealthy!

iUniverse books may be ordered through booksellers or by contacting:

iUniverse
2021 Pine Lake Road, Suite 100
Lincoln, NE 68512
www.iuniverse.com
1-800-Authors (1-800-288-4677)

Because of the dynamic nature of the Internet, any Web addresses or links contained in this book may have changed since publication and may no longer be valid.

ISBN: 978-0-595-42069-8 (pbk)
ISBN: 978-0-595-67971-3 (cloth)
ISBN: 978-0-595-86414-0 (ebk)

Printed in the United States of America

For my children, Chrissie, Mike, and Danny, who gave me the reason to persevere when the going got tough. For Joanne, Joe, and Ann, who proved that there are exceptions to every rule. For John, Mary, James, and Trish, the best siblings in the world. For Aunt Kay, who will always make me laugh. For Bobby, for daring me to succeed and being a great friend. For Nick, whose extraordinary help I am forever grateful for. For Mom, who gave me the courage never to give up. And for Dad, the kindest, sweetest man I ever knew. I am truly blessed.

CONTENTS

Part III: Getting Ahead: Having the Right Financial Plan

Introduction

If you find it difficult saving money, or even keeping your head above water in the financial sense, you are not alone. Most people I have met in my professional career who do not consider themselves wealthy are in similar financial circumstances. For a long time, I considered myself among this majority. I am of course referring to the average middle-class individual who works every day, at least forty hours a week, but finds it difficult to save money at the end of each month.

Many middle-class folks not only find it impossible to save money but also face the burden of accumulating credit card or consumer debt. Unfortunately, many middle-class people feel as if we are on a "financial wheel," where we work long hours during the month but, by the time the month is over, can barely cover bills with our hard-earned salaries.

For many years, I was exasperated with my own finances. After speaking with literally hundreds of people over twenty-two years, discussing and analyzing different circumstances over this period, I have concluded that most of us have similar financial difficulties. I have also discovered that these financial difficulties can be overcome, as the following pages will show. Please note that I speak from experience. Where once I struggled financially, now, with a different perspective, I have obtained financial stability, security, and confidence that I wish to share with you.

In order to share my opinions on how to "get ahead" financially, I explore why we *must* face financial difficulty. I explore our macro-economic society ("the big picture") and conclude that the folks with the most, the "rich," pretty much run the show. I explore why prices always rise, why and how our retirement plans have been systematically taken from us, the role our various media play in encouraging us to accept our fate, as well as the role of the national politician, who creates laws that perpetuate our struggle to "get ahead." Once you understand that you are *supposed to* struggle financially, I offer you a sound system for overcoming your financial difficulties. This book offers a unique approach to your finances by addressing why it is important that we struggle and what we can do about fixing our financial circumstances. I offer my opinions on investment opportunities, such as the stock market and investing in real estate, as well as a simple, solid approach to realistically plan and fund your retirement.

PART I

▼

THE ENSLAVEMENT OF THE MIDDLE CLASS: HOW IT WORKS

CHAPTER 1

▼

KEEPING THE MIDDLE CLASS DOWN: THE EXPENSE CONSTANT

"If everyone were rich, who would make me dinner?"

I remember laughing with a friend of mine (while my portfolio was tanking) as we discussed the downfall of the NASDAQ. In less than two years, the NASDAQ stock market had gone down almost 80 percent! I laughed because I was thinking of what the Federal Reserve chairman might have been saying as all these "dot-com" investors (investors who purchased stock of Internet companies) were becoming overnight multimillionaires. I imagined the chairman in a panic, because if his hired help became rich, they would not be there to make him dinner, and thus the chairman would be forced to fend for himself. This conversation was a form of therapeutic gallows humor. Like everyone else, I was losing my savings.

I imagined a scenario in which the chairman thought too many people were getting too rich, too quick—so he had to stop it. Immediately, the chairman set out to raise interest rates, causing the stock market to crumble and sending all the middle-class investors who had their life savings in the stock market from the penthouse to the out-house. Thus, the middle class stayed middle class, and in some cases dropped to the lower class. And wouldn't you know it—after the market crashed, the so-called experts on those cable financial channels all said the NASDAQ market was bound to crash, that the "bubble" was bound to burst. Funny, I don't recall those experts saying the NAS-DAQ stock market was going to crash before it went down 72 percent.

What does this story have to do with becoming wealthy and staying that way?

There are some lessons to learn from this stock market's rise and fall. Let's start with the basic notion that only a small percentage of people are monetarily wealthy compared to our total population. I think we can all agree on that. If you think about it, a whole bunch of people got super rich during the Nasdaq's rise. A whole bunch of non-rich people were becoming rich *really* fast. What would happen if everyone got rich? My guess is that if everyone were rich, being rich would not mean anything anymore. More importantly, if everyone were rich, no one would work. If no one worked, how could we eat, drive a car, or heat our homes? There would be no one left to work on the farm, no one left to work in the auto factory or gas station, no one left to work at the oil and heating companies.

See my point?

The rich have found a way to keep the rest of us scrambling for the table scraps: while the wealthy dole out little bits of money to us for our day's work, they get it all back, plus interest, by getting us to spend it before the day is even over!

You have to give those rich folks a lot of credit. They keep coming up with new reasons to raise prices, to pay us less than the rate of rising prices, and to get us to spend more and more of our wages on things we never used to spend money on. The recent phenomenon of the *kids' college tuition bill* is one example. Beginning in the early eighties, rich folks decided that it would be great to hook us parents on the idea that we should pay for our kids' college education. Well, that idea was *rich*. By convincing us (through media, television commercials, newspapers, etc.) that we should be paying for our kids' college education, they added at least a decade of work to our careers, meaning ten fewer retirement years. When I went to college, my dad (who was the kindest man I ever knew), said, "Good luck, son." That's it. My dad loved me with all of his heart, but paying for your child's education just wasn't the thing to do. After all, my dad and mom had the right to retire! They worked hard their whole lives and deserved to take it easy. So I paid for my education myself, and I believe I am a better person for it.

Fast-forward to today, when my kids cannot even get a significant student loan to pay for their education! The student loan has been reduced to almost nothing, while another method of paying for college has become the norm: the *parent loan*. This means even if I did not want to pay for my child's education, I'm forced to, because our politicians have decided that parents must now choose between retiring (and leaving our kids without an education) or working an extra decade to ensure our kids develop their minds in college. Of course, we are left without any real choice. We must work the extra decade.

It is a fact that a college graduate earns, on average, at least one million dollars more during her career than the average individual without a college degree. Since a college degree is financially harder to attain, I would argue that a smaller percentage of the population will receive a college degree, thus ensuring that a larger percentage of the population will remain in the working class. Data to support this argument includes the drastic reduction of government subsidies to colleges and students, such as the Pell Grant, which in the seventies comprised more than 70 percent of college funding but now makes up less than 30 percent of college funding. The individuals who make our laws, our politicians, are largely individuals of means; in other words, they are rich. Is it any wonder, then, that our politicians have passed laws over the past thirty years designed to reduce the number of individuals attaining college degrees?

Another recent item that we must now pay for is the *health insurance phenomena.* When I entered the workforce, health insurance was a virtually guaranteed employee benefit. Neither I nor anyone I worked with conceived that health insurance would be a monthly cost, tantamount to a home mortgage—and that we would be required to foot the bill! Those rich folk had struck again, raising monthly health insurance costs by more than twice the rate of inflation. The health insurance companies raise their rates because they claim they are "losing money." I too could claim I was "losing money" if I paid myself hundreds of millions of dollars in salary and called it a *business expense*. Then I could raise my premiums to cover my business expenses. The way I see it, we the working class just got hoodwinked by those rich folk—again. We pay more and more of our wages to cover "the rising cost of health insurance," when our money really goes into the pockets of the rich few who actually run the companies.

My guess is that the health insurance phenomenon has added another decade of work to our careers—that's another ten fewer years of retirement.

At this rate, I'll never retire! (That's exactly the point ...)

I've identified two additional expense burdens resulting in all of us fighting rush hour for an extra twenty years of our lives! But I have not even discussed the most expensive new burden—our *retirement*.

CHAPTER 2

▼

STRIPPING THE MIDDLE CLASS OF OUR RETIREMENT: THE 401(K) HOAX

Retirement. Wow. That's a biggie. Back in the day, when the Depression was the largest and worst socioeconomic memory, our ancestors took great pains to ensure that we would enjoy at least part of our lives as "retirees." Working every day for forty years meant a bit more when we knew we could take it easy for the remaining twenty or so years of our lives. I refer to this time in our history as the "golden years of the middle class," because we prioritized our need to retire, developing social security and the pension, whereby our employers set aside part of our salary for after our lifetime of labor.

Well, a funny thing happened on the way to retirement: the baby boom.

During this time, we witnessed the largest population growth in our history. Everyone seemed to be having babies from the late 1940s to the mid-1960s. The problem with producing so many babies in such a short time was that the time would come when a large percentage of the population would suddenly stop working, becoming retirees. The guardians of our society, the policy makers (the rich), figured out that our way of living could not support such a large segment of the population not working. There had to be a way to shorten this time of burden—the baby boom retirement years would have to be limited, and the concept of a formal retirement had to be changed to the concept of *semiretirement*. The concept of semiretirement was a brilliant way to lessen the burden and shock to the economy of such a large number of people retiring all at once. The only problem with semiretirement is that by implementing this methodology, a large portion of our population may never actually retire. The situation has gotten so bad that I foresee a future constitutional amendment worded as follows:

All individuals of this great country have the right to a lengthy and prosperous retirement. In accordance with this God-given, inalienable right, we hereby amend to Constitution of the United States of America to set forth, from this day forward, a mandatory Age of Retirement. Such an Age of Retirement shall be consistent with the age of all people, regardless of race, creed, sex, or sexual orientation, to be mandatory at the age commencing on the anniversary of the fifth year subsequent to an individual's mortem. This amendment to our Constitution will guarantee a peaceful retirement for all of the citizens of this great United States of America in the life we live in the hereafter.

Of course, I can see a legal disclaimer added to such an amendment:

Results of this constitutional amendment may vary. Not responsible for acts of badness perpetrated by an individual that may dictate the final location of one's resting place, be it heaven or hell. We do, however, recommend bringing some fire resistant clothing to the latter destination.

Seriously, folks, there has been a systematic dismantling of the retirement concept since the early 1980s. Since then, "alternative retirement plans," such as 401(k) plans and profit-sharing plans, have become the replacement for the traditional pension plan. Gradually, the protectors of the traditional pension plan, the *union*, have been ridiculed and marginalized by the media. It was a stroke of genius to portray the union as a membership of lazy, overpaid thugs who wished only to bleed society of its resources. Think about it—how many times have you read about a union and its connection to organized crime?

Without the social influence of the union to remind us continually that we need to protect ourselves from the rich, we have systematically lost our rights to a traditional pension. The pension system has eroded to the point where we are now being brainwashed into thinking that the once undeniable right to social security is in jeopardy of bankruptcy. New proposals, such as "individual private investment accounts," have been floated by politicians to replace the concept of the traditional social security benefit. The notion of "security" as part of social security is being dismantled right before our very eyes! Even though politicians (whose health insurance premiums are paid for the duration of their lives) have guaranteed traditional pensions, they have increasingly passed legislation making the traditional pension plan obsolete while simultaneously providing tax incentives to business owners to cultivate alternative pension plans, such as 401(k) and profit-sharing retirement plans.

What's so bad about an alternative pension plan?

Despite the fancy names of these alternative pension plans, they are, by themselves, insufficient to provide a meaningful pension for the retiree. The problem is, not too many people seem to realize the realistic cost of a pension plan. Let me give you an example: Let's say twenty years from now you want to retire. How much money, on a yearly basis, do you think you would need? Average increases in inflation added to today's cost of living would mean an average couple should need approximately $80,000 per year to live in reasonable comfort. So, the question you must ask yourself is, "How much money do I need to have saved in the bank in order to receive $80,000 per year worth of interest?"

Well, first you have to figure out a reasonable rate of return on your money in the bank. Over a long term, say twenty years, committing to a 5 percent annual interest return on your investment is reasonable. You likely won't be putting your money at risk if you seek only a 5 percent rate of return, so let's assume your money is safe. Using these assumptions, if I want $80,000 per year in interest, and my money earns 5 percent per year, I must therefore save a total of $1,600,000 for my retirement!

There are many types of alternative pension plan, but for the sake of simplicity, let's assume the average alternative pension plan permits you to save up to 10 percent of your salary, with the company matching that benefit. If you contributed to your pension for twenty years and averaged $80,000 per year in salary, you would contribute a total of $16,000 per year towards your pension ($8,000 by you and $8,000 by your employer). What would the value of a $16,000 dollar annual contribution (at 5 percent per year interest) be twenty years into the future? The answer is $529,055. If you wanted to live off the interest only, you would receive a pension of only $26,452.

Now, let's say you worked for your company for thirty years and contributed the same $16,000 per year. The future value of an annuity of $16,000 per year at 5 percent for thirty years would be $1,063,021. If you wanted to live off the interest only, at 5 percent per year, you would receive a pension of only $53,151.

What annual salary then, working for a company for twenty years, would it take to receive a pension of $80,000 per year? The answer is a whopping $241,940! What annual salary would you need to earn to receive a pension of $80,000 per year if you worked for a company for thirty years? You would need to average an annual salary of $120,411! What "average Joe" averages $241,940 per year in wages for twenty years, or $120,411 for thirty years, working for a company?

I have provided this example to illustrate how difficult it is to fund a pension. There are other methods of calculating pension funding, including actuarial tables and other mechanisms, whereby the actual principle balance of the pension is calculated to be reduced to zero at your death. I do not include such tables, since it is possible to outlive the actuarial tables, and in such a case, your $80,000 per year benefit would not be guaranteed.

In short, the alternative pension plan is, by itself, woefully insufficient to meet our financial obligations during our retirement years. Contrast this to the concept of the traditional pension plan, where the common benefit is 75 percent of your last five years' average annual salary—in this case you would need to earn an average of $106,666 for the last five years prior to retirement. It is conceivable that twenty years from now, the average salary per individual in the workplace with twenty years' experience will be $106,666. And the best part of the traditional pension plan is that it does not cost the employee anything—it is a company-paid benefit!

Now, wouldn't it make sense for the rich, if they did not want us to retire, to change how our pensions are funded? I believe it does make sense, and, as illustrated above, *I believe they have!*

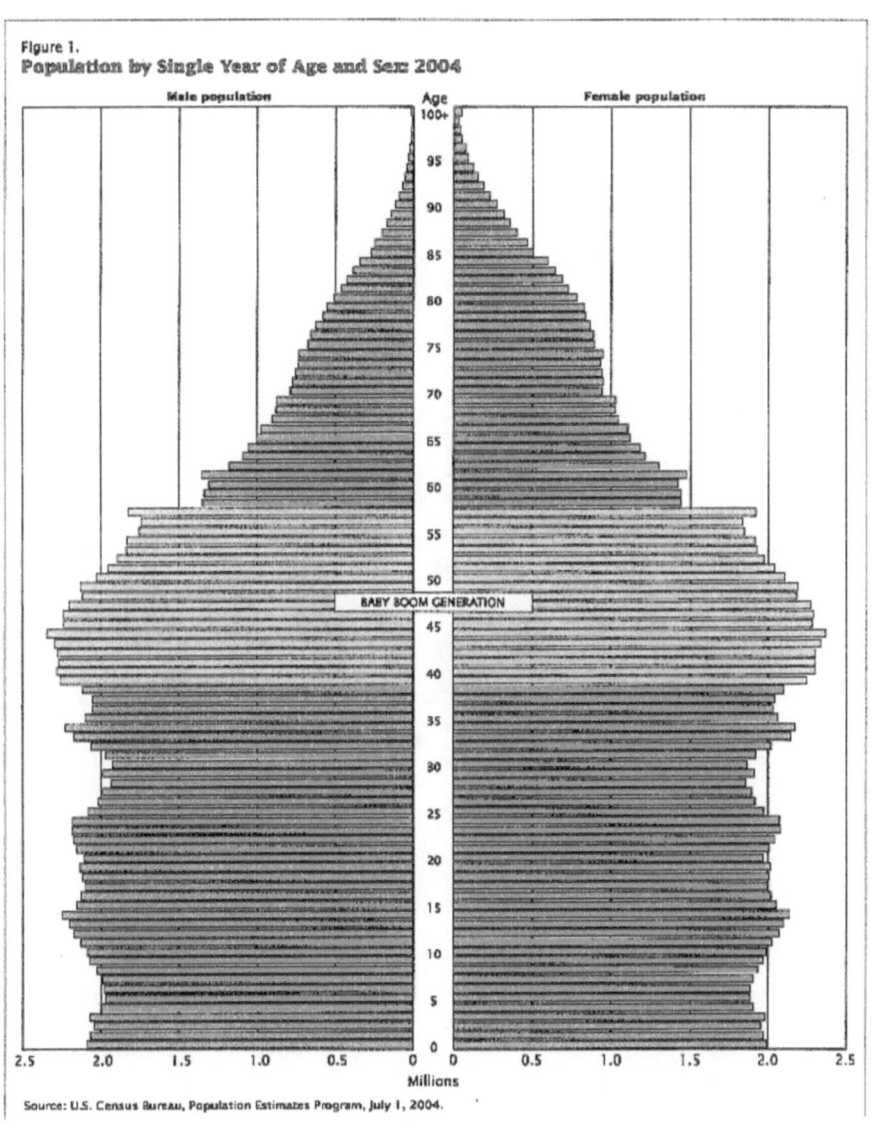

Figure 1.
Population by Single Year of Age and Sex: 2004

The problem: Who is going to fill the jobs left by a baby boom generation retirement class? Note that this chart clearly indicates this potential problem. The answer: Eliminate retirement!

CHAPTER 3

▼

CAN'T "GET AHEAD"? THANK UNCLE SAM!

The mechanism that the rich use to keep themselves rich and to keep the rest of us working every day is our government itself. By passing laws that tax us literally to death, they ensure that if we are not careful, we will never get ahead.

How is this possible?

The first thing we have to deal with is the illusion that the average working family earning $100,000 per year is rich. If you live in an area where the cost of living is low, you might actually have a few bucks left over at the end of the year. However, if you live in a place where the cost of living is high (e.g., New York, California, Hawaii), keeping your head above financial water is not guaranteed even with this income. The government, however, says that if you earn such an annual sum, you are rich, and therefore you must pay a larger percentage of your wages to the government in income taxes.

Let's look at an illustration, based on today's tax rates, for a New York State family (husband/wife/two kids/dog):

TABLE 3.1 Income and Expenses for a Typical New York State Family

Income	
Gross income	$100,000
Taxes	
Federal income tax	($7,929)
Child tax credit (if kids under 17)	$2,000
Net federal income tax	($5,929)
Net NYS income tax (not NYC/Yonkers)	($4,378)
Net real estate tax (L.I. only)	($6,500)
Net social security tax paid (2004)	($5,450)
Net Medicare tax paid	($1,450)
Net sales tax paid (L.I. only)	($2,625)
Total taxes paid	($26,332)
Net income	**$73,668**

TABLE 3.1 Income and Expenses for a Typical New York State Family (Continued)

Expenses	
Mortgage payment	$15,700
Homeowners insurance	$1,000
Home heating costs	$2,000
Health insurance premiums (50 percent employer paid)	$6,000
Electricity	$3,600
Automobile payments (2)	$7,200
Automobile insurance (2 cars)	$3,600
Cable/Internet	$1,000
Food	$13,000
Clothing	$5,000
Commuting/travel/gasoline	$5,000
401(k) contribution	$10,000
Credit card interest	$10,000
Contributions	$1,500
Entertainment/vacations/miscellaneous	$12,000
Total expenses	**$96,600**
Total income	**$73,668**
Total expenses	**$96,600**
Net surplus (deficit) for year	**($22,932)**

Now, I ask, can you compare the net taxes paid for the year with the net deficit for the year? Are they remarkably close?

You now know that when a politician says he wants to increase taxes on the rich, he means the folks making $100,000 per year. Let's assume the above family rents a home. According to our tax laws, the people who cannot afford to purchase a home receive the benefit of actually paying more income taxes. Rent is not a deductible expense on your federal or NYS personal income tax return. Therefore, if you take away real estate tax and mortgage interest as a deduction, your federal income tax for the year would *increase* 38 percent, from $7,929 to $10,956! Your NYS income tax would increase from $4,378 to $4,919, an increase of 12.4 percent. Your net deficit would increase $3,568 to an astonishing $32,500 per year. This deficit increase assumes your monthly rent expense does not exceed your monthly mortgage, which in this calculation is $1,850.

Critics may say the above illustration is incorrect, because families don't incur nearly $23,000 per year in debt. The reason family annual debt may not increase by nearly $23,000 per year, in my view, is that families realize they must make cuts to curtail their household expenses.

Generally, the first cut is the pension contribution, while the next fall in the vacations and miscellaneous categories. Making these drastic cuts in our household expenses still leaves the average household in a deficit, albeit not as large. My point is, in spite of earning a household income of $100,000 per year, if you live in New York State (Long Island, specifically), you are *not rich*. The government and the media would have us all think otherwise.

The above calculation is a dramatic argument that the family that does not have the means to purchase a home pays more in taxes than the family that has the means to purchase a home. Therefore, I would argue that the system of taxing people is inversely correlated to the assets we are able to accumulate in our lifetime. The fewer assets we accumulate in our lifetime, the fewer tax shelters (or ways to reduce our tax burden) we'll have in our lifetime. The moral of the story should be to accumulate assets during our lifetime in order to pay less tax throughout our lifetime.

I would argue further, based on the above illustration, that our system of taxation is designed to ensure that we spend a lifetime working, with no expectation of retirement—if we are not careful!

CHAPTER 4

THE REAL REASON
PRICES RISE

Why does the cost of everything we spend our wages on always seem to go up?

The answer to this basic question is, in my view, the foundation of our *economic internal machine*.

If prices did not rise, we would be able to save more of our wages over time and possibly—I dare say—"get ahead." When you get a job and work at it for a while, chances are you get better at it. If you get better at something you are getting paid for, chances are you will command a higher wage from your boss. You get paid a higher wage from your boss not just because you are getting better but because when you get better, you usually become more productive. If you become more productive, your boss makes more money from your productivity. If, over time, you make more wages, you may actually save some of it and be able to retire (and you know the rich can't have that). The answer for the rich, then, is to come up with new reasons why you must give your increased wages back to them even before they get to the bank. To keep the game known as our *daily economy* going, and to continually throw us off our financial game plan, retail prices for all items rise, one at a time.

Picture, if you will, a baseball team named the United States Inflation All-Star Team, with a star-studded lineup of power hitters. Imagine the announcer introducing each player over the P.A. system: *"Batting leadoff for the United States Inflation All-Star Team, Oil Prices. Batting second, and leading the league in stolen money from your pockets, Health Insurance Premiums! Batting third, and leading the league in runs and money scored, Electricity Prices! Batting fourth, our heavy hitter, the all-time home run king in the economy's history, Interest Rates!"*

Imagine, now, a full lineup of various costs we encounter in our daily lives, all rising at different times and with creative new reasons as to why they are rising!

My favorite *reason* economic experts use to justify rising commodity prices is what I like to call the "China syndrome." When the price of something like oil goes up, or the price of steel rises, I hear the old standby, "It's China's fault." Economists and the folks that "analyze" the fluctuation of rising prices seem to love blaming China when something rises in price. *"Well, you see, China is the largest populated country in the world, and because they have so many people, they keep using more and more of the world's supply of natural resources, and so steel prices must go higher … "* Etcetera, etcetera.

Then there's the other doozy: *"Sheetrock prices have increased by 20 percent this week because we now have a tree shortage in the northwest corridor of the United States, where most trees are located for sheetrock production."*

A tree shortage?

That's a good one.

We all know about the excuses used repeatedly to justify rising oil prices. Sometimes economists say it's China's fault, sometimes they say it's because of the continuing unrest in the Middle East, and sometimes they say it's because we don't have enough refineries running to process oil into gasoline.

Why, then, I ask these "economists," was the price of oil only $9 per barrel in 1999, while only five years later, in 2005, oil prices rose to a crazy $68 per barrel? Has the world changed so much in five years that the price of any item should rise more than 750 percent?

There is simply no justification for the rise in the price of any commodity other than the real reason: to keep us working longer in terms of the workday and the work life. All other reasons you hear are just excuses. Think about it. We've got some of the brightest minds in the world researching things in the area of nuclear physics, bimolecular sciences, and a host of other medical and technological fields. We can place an object into space and determine its landing point to within a few feet 35 million miles from Earth. We have identified the human genome and the amazing science that comes from biomedicine. Yet, despite our brilliance, we cannot come up with an automobile that runs on something other than gasoline, the byproduct of oil?

Does anyone really believe this?

If you watch informational television shows such as those on the Science Channel, the Discovery Channel, etc., it seems that once a month there is a television show depicting yet another vehicle that runs on something other than gasoline. Yet, why don't we see these products on the market? It would seem that if these types of vehicles were actually on the market, we could reduce our need for oil products. By reducing our need for oil products, we would not be subject to the generational squeeze that the rise in the price of oil subjects us to. Further exploration into why these oil-free products don't make it to the market would most likely lead to a conclusion that somehow, the oil and automobile industries are working together in stifling such innovation, thus rendering us helpless to combat the ridiculous rises in oil prices.

I do not claim to be a man of science, but common sense tells me that we have renewable, natural resources available to all of us, such as solar energy, that we can use as a substitute for gasoline to power our vehicles. How difficult would it be to mass produce solar panels and install them on top of our vehicles to capture solar energy? This energy—continuous, clean, and free of charge—is a viable alternative to the insane costs of gasoline-powered vehicles. I believe this technology exists—it is simple, sound, and relatively inexpensive. Why have we not seen such technology incorporated into automobiles? Likely because the wealthy—in this case, the oil companies around the world—would suffer if such technology were implemented. If automobile companies created a vehicle that operated primarily on solar energy, the oil companies would put them out of business. How? Simple. Auto companies are traded publicly on stock exchanges. It would not be difficult for the oil companies to short sell the stock of the auto companies repeatedly until they drove their prices down to zero. In essence, automobile manufacturers need to keep producing gasoline-powered vehicles to stay in business.

Who controls the trading markets?

Traders trade on behalf of their clients, who themselves bid the price of oil up or down. *In effect, the price of oil is determined by the clients of the exchange traders all over the world, not by OPEC, Middle East concerns, or any other scapegoats that the media gives us.* So then, who are the clients of the traders of oil futures that dictate the price of oil? My guess is that, although this is impossible to prove, the big hand of Big Oil is there somewhere, pushing the price of oil upwards by bidding up the price of oil futures, as the client of the oil trader.

Remember, machinery of all types are run by oil. So, if the price of oil goes up, the price of everything we buy goes up. How great is that—to be able to control the price of a single commodity and therefore control the price of almost all things we buy? It's brilliant. *It's rich!*

CHAPTER 5

▼

FINANCIAL CATASTROPHE FOR THE MIDDLE CLASS: LOW INTEREST RATES

Interest rate fluctuations are my favorite character in the plot to keep us working. I love this character because of the counterintuitive effects of high and low interest rates. In other words, you might think that low interest rates work to your advantage. I would argue that low interest rates work entirely against your efforts to get ahead.

Let me preface my theory with a question. Who controls the interest rates we pay our creditors or the interest we earn on our savings accounts? I would argue it is the body of member banks known as the Federal Reserve. What? I know, I just implied "banks" and "Federal Reserve" were a related entity. How could a group of bankers be the Federal Reserve? Because the Federal Reserve is not a government entity but rather a *quasi-government entity*! Imagine, naming your business the Federal Reserve and getting people to think you are part of the government! The member banks of the Federal Reserve are privately controlled corporations, not our government.

Take it a step further and ask, "What title do the heads of the different groups have within the Federal Reserve?" The answer is "governor." Of course, the title of the board that raises and lowers interest rates on the Federal Reserve is the "Board of Governors." These folks are technically government employees, but they answer to their members—the member banks! By including the word "Federal" in its name and giving the title of "governor" to its directors, the Reserve gives itself instant credibility. We even go as far as having our Senate confirm the hiring of the chairman of the Federal Reserve, who is nominated by the President of our country. Now that's some serious credibility! (Personally, I think it's another stroke of genius by those rich folks.)

In short, the folks that control interest rates are not truly related to the government but rather serve the interests of the member banks, which are owned and operated by the super-rich. These characters get together periodically to decide whether to raise or lower interest rates. Their decisions affect all of us, because these are the people who control the supply of money lent to banks and the interest rate to charge member banks, who in turn lend it to us. So, if the Board of Governors decides to lower interest rates, they do so to the commercial banks, which in turn lower interest rates that they charge us for things like mortgages, credit cards, etc.

My outline of this process is a simplified—I could get really technical about money supply issues, etc.—but accurate characterization of the basics of the system.

How can low interest rates be bad?

If interest rates are low, people are more inclined to borrow and put themselves into debt. If you put yourself into debt, you are less inclined to get ahead.

Interest rates determine the cost of the most expensive single purchase we make in our lifetimes—the purchase of our homes. In order to survive on this earth, we need three basic things, food, clothing, and shelter. Since we live in a country blessed with fruitful land, food can be obtained at a relatively low cost. Clothing can also be obtained at a relatively low cost. Therefore, if all we have left is the cost of shelter to survive, I would argue that it's (shelter) got to be really expensive, otherwise we would not have an incentive to get out there and work! The balance must be just right. Shelter has to be attainable, but it must require a lifetime of labor to attain. That's where a thirty-year mortgage comes in. A thirty-year mortgage guarantees we will have to work for thirty years to pay off our debt. What a concept!

Here is where low interest rates really hurt our efforts to get ahead. The cost of shelter is dictated by the rate of interest we must pay to the bank each month. My experience has told me that the majority of people purchase homes not by the total purchase price of the home but by the monthly cost. We seem to focus on the monthly burden of paying our mortgage and therefore look to pay what we can afford each month. I would argue that the single reason why the cost of shelter has tripled over the last four years is that the Federal Reserve lowered interest rates to historically low levels.

Most people set aside a certain amount each month for their mortgage payment before they actually purchase a home. When planning the purchase, most people figure out what they can pay monthly and borrow what they can to make that payment. If interest rates are low, we can borrow more money to make the same payment. Armed with the ability to borrow more money, we have actually raised the cost of our house purchase by making higher offers during the bidding process of purchasing a home. The frenzy of rising prices for shelter has occurred because of the ability to borrow more money at the same monthly cost. Keeping our monthly cost the same is a direct result of lower interest rates.

Using my own residence as an indicator, prices for the most expensive purchase in our lifetime, our home, have tripled from 2001 to 2005. Have three times the amount of purchasers entered the housing market? Nope. Has the supply of houses suddenly dried up? Nope. I would argue that both the supply of and the demand for houses have remained relatively constant. Looking our aging population, one can conclude that the disproportionate demand for housing baby boomers ended on or about 1990, resulting in the stagnation of housing prices in the decade that followed. Inasmuch as the generation subsequent to the baby boomers is smaller in numbers, housing demand based on population cannot be greater today than when

baby boomers were buying homes. (This conclusion is cor-
roborated by the population graph supplied by the US
Census Bureau, page 12.) The only thing that has changed
significantly in this game is that we have more money
available to pay for a home, thus creating a bidding war on
the price of houses, resulting in the incredibly high prices
we see today.

Wow! These folks at the Federal Reserve are clever. *All
they had to do was tweak interest rates, and we did the rest!*

The flipside of borrowing more is that the Federal
Reserve has created, with its reduction in interest rates, a
dis-incentive to save money. What good is it to save money
when you receive a very small rate of return on your investment? In other words, why put whatever savings you can
muster in the bank and receive maybe 2 percent interest
income on your investment when you can buy a house
with that money (and a loan, of course) and maybe double
or triple your money?

Well, that's all well and good provided you purchase a
home at a low price and sell at a higher price. This type of
investing requires market timing, something that would
make us all rich if we all possessed it. But this is not an easy
thing to do. Additionally, you take a very large risk when
investing in any venture with borrowed money, because if

the investment goes bad, your liability can exceed the amount of your investment.

I would argue that the individuals safeguarding monetary policy (interest rates) do not offer a reasonable rate of return in a savings account because they *do not want us to save money*—thus, once again, making the retirement option not an option at all.

By not offering a reasonable rate of return on our savings, the low-interest-rate policy has hurt another segment of our population—*senior citizens.* After saving their wages over a lifetime, many seniors rely on the earnings of their savings accounts to pay their monthly expenses. By lowering interests rates dramatically, the Federal Reserve has drastically cut the monthly income of senior citizens, who rely on their earnings from their savings accounts. Assuming over the past five years that the typical savings account has reduced its interest rate of return from 5 percent to 2 percent, we can argue that the typical annual interest earnings from a savings account have been reduced by 60 percent! For any segment of the population to absorb a 60-percent reduction in annual income—especially in a climate of rising prices—is a travesty. Seniors caught in this web of monetary policy will be forced out of retirement and back into the workforce. Can anyone say *semiretirement?*

On the other hand, wealthy bankers prosper enormously from low interest rates. As illustrated above, the banks have typically cut their interest expense by 60 percent, because they typically pay out 60 percent less on the earnings of their customer's savings accounts. The typical mortgage paid to banks five years ago was approximately 8 percent. Today, banks are lending money at a rate of 5.5 percent. If we look at the comparison of lower mortgage interest revenues that banks receive, we see only a percentage decrease of 31.25 percent, yet the rates banks pay out to their customers have decreased 60 percent. This has resulted in dramatically higher profits. For example, Citicorp's annual net income rose from $ 14.13 billion in 2001 to $ 24.59 billion in 2005, a 74 percent increase in annual net income. In 2006, the effects of rising interest rates resulted in a net decrease in Citicorp's net income to $ 21.54 billion—a startling 12.4 percent decline in net income.

Who gets hurt by low interest rates?

- *Young adults.* They are encouraged to borrow more and generally must save their wages for a longer period in order to accumulate enough money for a larger down payment for a home.

- *Parents of young adults (middle age).* Parents must provide housing for their children for a much longer period, and in many cases they are now finding themselves in the position of contributing their wages to their children's down payment costs. In addition, not receiving a reasonable rate of return on their retirement plans effectively forces parents of young adults to work many more years than previous generations.

- *Senior citizens.* The most dramatically affected by low interest rate policy, senior citizens must absorb a dramatic cut in income in an environment of rising prices.

Low interest rates enable more people to borrow more money

If people have more money available to spend on items (such as in the example of rising real estate prices), then prices will rise to meet the increased level of money people have access to spend. Accordingly, in my view, *interest rates are the primary cause of inflation.*

I would argue that the only group of people who benefit from low interest rates are the wealthy, while the rest of us suffer financially from low interest rate policies. Is this really a surprise to anyone?

PART II

▼

THE AGENTS OF ENSLAVEMENT: THE MEDIA AND THE POLITICIAN

CHAPTER 6

▼

THE NATIONAL MEDIA: SELLING THE MIDDLE CLASS ITS FATE

It might have occurred to you that even though this money stuff is not that difficult to understand, have we not seen much about these things in the newspaper or on television news programs. While we have seen these issues in the various media, they have been framed to produce a different point of view.

You may not be aware that laws governing the ownership of media outlets (newspapers, television stations) have changed. Previously, the law prohibited media outlets from owning numerous other media outlets, so that we could maintain a wide spectrum of opinions on all matters. Today, those barriers have been lifted. As a result, a relatively few mega-corporations now own all of our major media outlets. When we receive our news and opinions from just one collective source, we read and hear a point of view framed to encourage us to believe what the media wants us to believe. Who owns these media outlets that create and shape what we read and hear? You guessed it—the wealthy.

Do you think the media is going to address, fairly, both sides of interest rates? Of course not. The media tells us that low interest rates are good, selling the idea that you pay less. Always selling. Always pounding the same message. What you won't find in the newspapers you read or the television reports you watch is the true picture: that low interest rates cause the prices of everything to go up. When was the last time you read an article in the newspaper that stated our pensions have been taken from us and that this is a bad thing? You won't find such an article or television news report, because the wealthy have taken our pensions away and the wealthy control our media. What you will find, however, are newspaper articles and television shows deriding pensions as a bad thing. This is because pension costs are so expensive that our poor mega-corporations cannot compete with companies that do not provide pension plans and therefore must fire their employees. Conveniently, these same newspaper articles and television news reports don't tell you that our mega-corporations are competing against businesses, primarily overseas, that pay slave wages to their "employees." It is my opinion, the fact that we are competing against businesses we never used to compete against is simply an excuse to take away our pensions.

Years ago, our country protected itself and our workers by charging a tariff, or tax, against overseas business that produced inexpensive goods on the backs of slave labor. This policy was a way for our economy to level the playing field, to provide a way for our businesses to compete. Our politicians have since passed legislation eliminating or reducing these tariffs. An example of such legislation is the North American Free Trade Agreement (NAFTA), passed in 1992, which drastically reduced tariffs between the United States and Mexico. The effect of such legislation provides a basis for the mega-corporation to take away our pensions. I bet you don't read or see this part of the pension issue in the mainstream media, i.e., television, print, and radio!

My favorite spin on the pension debate is the one my local paper (owned by one of those mega-corporations) loves to churn out repeatedly. The editors have compiled a series of newspaper articles selling the notion that it is unfair that government workers have pension plans while private sector employees do not. The newspaper's solution is not outrage at the fact that the majority of the working class have lost their pensions but rather that some government employees still receive them. Incredibly, the newspaper has twisted the fundamental topic of this issue completely around. Yet it should not surprise us that such a simple issue has been twisted to hurt the working folks. After all, who owns the media outlets? The mega-corporations. Who owns the mega-corporations? The wealthy. The moral of the story: whenever you read an article, read an editorial, or see a television news story, consider the source.

The media has taken the next step of creating a financial television channel that continuously promotes the idea that pensions are a terrible thing, health care coverage is a terrible thing, and poor mega-corporations cannot survive with such benefit, or legacy costs, for their workers. This same financial television channel interviews economists who tell us repeatedly that high interest rates are a terrible thing for our economy. Their reasoning goes even further: since high interest rates are terrible for our economy, they say, when interest rates rise, our mega-corporations will make less money. If our mega-corporations make less money, the value of the mega-corporation goes down.

The value of the mega-corporation is reflected in the price of its stock, which, following this reasoning, goes down in value. Where are our 401(k) retirement plans invested? The stock market. What happens when interest rates rise? Stock prices fall. What happens to our 401(k) plans? They shrink. Who controls the trading of stocks? The wealthy. Therefore, in effect, if we raise our interest rates, the wealthy will take our money from our 401(k) plan. What does this tell us? Primarily, it tells us to stay away from the stock market, but more importantly, it tells us that the media has sold us on the idea that low interest rates are bad—and if you don't believe them, just look at your 401(k) plan!

Have you noticed that the cost of housing tripled from 2001 to 2005? Have you noticed that your grocery bill has doubled over the last five years? Have you noticed that your electric bill has increased 50 percent in the last five years? Have you noticed that your health insurance premium has double in the last five years? And have you noticed that your salary has risen, if you are lucky, maybe 25 percent in the last five years? Notice the big problem here? I notice, the working folks that I talk to notice, so why does the media say, over and over, that "there is no inflation," and that "inflation is under control"? How do such obvious, clear issues escape notice when the media produces their programs? The answer is simple. The media has elected to repeat the same thing until we give up our intelligent criticisms and believe what they are feeding us. The psychology of group thinking is evident here, whereby the individual is bound to agree with a large group, even if the group is clearly wrong.

We hear, repeatedly, the words *freedom* and *capitalism* and *free markets* from these financial television channels. They use words that represent wonderful concepts as catch phrases to sell the ideas that the media wants us to believe. But we need to understand that the media are owned by the wealthy, and as such, we receive the messages the wealthy want us to receive. The growing presence of the Internet as a viable media outlet provides an enlightening alternative to the monopoly of today's mainstream media. I recommend that you search the Internet for varying perspectives on the issues I discuss to further enhance your view of the subject matter. The Internet, if used correctly, is an invaluable resource for information.

CHAPTER 7

▼

THE NATIONAL POLITICIAN: SELLING THE MIDDLE CLASS DOWN THE RIVER

The next great salespeople in our daily lives are our politicians. When the word *politician* is spoken, a typical response these days in one of disgust. Why? Because politicians, as a group, have earned such a reaction. Yet, why do we repeatedly hire people we don't trust (with our votes) to make laws governing the way we live our lives? This is a paradox I have yet to understand. I do, however, see these politicians, with help from the media, selling themselves to us via newspaper advertisements, mailings, and television commercials. I am sure you are aware that such media advertisements are extremely expensive. Who pays for such expenses? Obviously, people who donate money to the politicians' campaigns. Who donates money to the politicians' campaign? Largely, the huge sums of money originate from the bank accounts of mega-corporations. Who owns the mega-corporation? The wealthy. Therefore, we can logically conclude that, primarily, the wealthy buy their way into our government by sponsoring a *winning* politician. Is it then any surprise that our laws, enacted by politicians, have a decided benefit for the wealthy?

It's a thing of beauty watching how politicians keep our attention diverted from rich folks' assault on the middle class. Politicians accomplish this by creating issues that, although important, have absolutely nothing to do with our financial security. In other words, while keeping us distracted with issues such as family values, same-sex marriage, and illegal immigration, politicians are passing volumes of new laws designed to keep us enslaved to our jobs for the duration of our lifetimes. It's incredible how these politicians can champion a particular side of these issues so fervently while not one of them has screamed outrage at the systematic dismantling of the middle class and the opportunities that have been removed from the baby boom generation. It is a sad commentary that families can be divided down the middle on social issues but cannot seem to comprehend that these issues have been specifically designed to throw us off track from what is really going on—the removal of hope, retirement, and financial security from the middle class as a whole.

Let's set the record straight once and for all—social issues are incredibly important, but these issues take a back seat to the financial security of those of us who reside in the middle class.

The message we must send to our politicians is this: Give us back hope—for our financial lives and our retirement. Only then we can deal with these other issues.

Social security

Recently, I saw an amazing alliance of media and politics. Our mega-corporate–owned local newspaper published a series of articles vilifying government workers who receive pensions. Capitalizing on the issue, a politician who wants to become governor of our state decided that he would make this issue the reason we should give our vote to him. This politician has pledged to eliminate pension plans for newly hired government workers and replace the pension with a 401(k) plan. By eliminating pension plans for government workers, we will have successfully eliminated hope for last sector of our working class that has held on to the concept of retirement. It is my view that this media-shaped issue has gained in popularity, and it is only a matter of time before the traditional pension plan is taken away from the government worker. You will see literally hundreds of television and newspaper articles feigning outrage at the concept of the government worker earning a traditional pension. Eventually, we will fall victim to this media-induced, wealth-driven rhetoric, which will lead to the extinguishment of the government pension. Who will make this happen? The same politician that has been bought and sold by the mega-corporation.

Politicians and the media, collectively, have convinced us that social security is financially unstable.

As a people, we expect—because we have been told so repeatedly—that social security will become insolvent. No money left. It will be the politician, with the blessing and encouragement of the media, who eventually takes away this tiny stipend that represented a lifetime of work.

Remember, we all have paid 12.4 percent of our lifetime wages into social security. How can such large amounts, billions and billions of dollars, not be available for retirement? *My view is that our social security will not be available because the wealthy do not want social security to exist in the future.*

It was the politician who changed the laws concerning bankruptcy. Bankruptcy is the legal proceeding one enters when he has made mistakes regarding his finances. In the past, an individual was able to ask the court for relief of debts owed to his creditors. A person was permitted to show the court the financial dilemma he created, and the court, in the majority of cases, excused the debt to give the individual a new start in his financial life. Thanks to the politician, this *avenue is no longer available to the majority of working people.* The law has changed to require a person's annual income as well as a person's employment status to be the determining factor in whether one can seek bankruptcy relief from the court. In addition, the new bankruptcy legislation requires a complex maze of paperwork to be completed by the individual seeking relief, causing attorney fees to increase dramatically. How does creating additional attorney fees help the individual filing for bankruptcy (who is filing because he has no money to begin with)? The increased legal fees alone prohibit many from seeking bankruptcy relief—they simply can't pay for it! A study released on CNBC in November 2006 analyzing the effectiveness of the "new bankruptcy rules" in their first year showed that bankruptcy filings were down a stunning 95 percent from the year previous; of the 5 remaining percent that did file, 70 percent of these filings were stalled for one reason or another.

Suffice it to say, the average working person will never be entitled to such relief, because the income level of the average person is too high to excuse the average debt in a bankruptcy proceeding. The result is that should the average person plunge into debt, there is no realistic way to start anew. The average person is married to his financial mistakes for a lifetime. The funny thing is, these new laws surrounding bankruptcy proceedings do not affect the mega-corporation.

Surprised? You shouldn't be.

Medicare

It will be the politician who changes our laws regarding Medicare. Medicare is our national supplemental medical insurance program, which protects our senior citizens from financial catastrophe when they become sick. By protecting our senior citizens from financial catastrophe, we are able to protect the assets of our seniors, assets that will eventually be handed down to their children in the form of an inheritance. By inheriting wealth, a working person can retire more comfortably. As I said earlier, I believe that *the wealthy will implement every tool at their disposal to see that we do not have the opportunity to retire.*

By sponsoring the politician to enact laws that will limit Medicare participation and benefits, the politician will do the bidding of the wealthy. The media will create newspaper articles and television news coverage focusing on the failure to properly finance the Medicare program, using buzzwords like "entitlement" to create and sell the fiction that this program is not a benefit to the working person.

Entitlement is an important buzzword among media and politicians, who use it to frame government programs as charity for the poor. The term gives the listener the impression that these programs are just charities for the poor, when in fact they are designed to be programs that *we have paid for.* Since we have all paid into these programs, we have the right to demand the government either return the money we invested—with interest—or provide the payments and services we spent a lifetime paying for. By calling these programs "entitlements," our politicians and media have manipulated the English language to twist the facts surrounding the issues and to convince us that we are not *entitled* to get our money back.

Once the media sells this idea to the public, politicians *will* change the law to limit our benefits from Medicare. This will be the final step towards creating a working middle class that will be without the benefit of an inheritance and possibility without retirement.

Senior citizens' assets will be seized to pay for medical bills left uncovered by the revised Medicare program. And remember bankruptcy? Not an option anymore. Effectively, estates passed on to our children will exist only for the wealthy. Any assets we accumulate throughout our working lives will no longer be passed down to our children but rather used up to pay for our medical expenses.

The liquidation of the estates of the middle class is happening today: as the cost of health insurance skyrocket for older people who have not reached the age of Medicare, paying these premiums literally requires liquidating one's assets. In many states, premiums are determined by risk factors, including age. The liquidation of the individual's assets to pay such premiums foreshadows the eventual demise of the Medicare program, and as such the demise of the estates of the middle class.

Is it any surprise that there is presently a movement by our politicians to eliminate the estate tax? The estate tax is designed to fund our society by taxing the estates of wealthy individuals who pass away with tremendous fortunes. By repealing the estate tax, the wealthy will stay wealthy, while the working class will have no estate left to inherit, because it will have been consumed by medical bills.

PART III

▼

GETTING AHEAD: HAVING THE RIGHT FINANCIAL PLAN

CHAPTER 8

▼

FIGHTING BACK: YOUR NEW FINANCIAL PLAN— DESTROY YOUR DEBT AND SAVE!

We've covered the why and the how of not being able to "get ahead." Now let us look at the what, as in, "What we can do to overcome the hurdles that keep us struggling financially?"

You know why your parents were smart? They were raised in an era when the now-famous Depression of the late 1920s was more than just a story told at bedtime. No, your parents, for the most part, actually lived through those impoverished times. Living through such difficult times taught our parents the value of saving money.

Our parents and grandparents found out the hard way that nobody was going to take care of them but themselves. As such, our parents and grandparents made sure that they elected politicians who passed laws designed to actually help the middle class, not impoverish them.

Our parents and grandparents understood the value of organized labor and collectively insisted on things like a pension plan and social security. Our parents and grandparents were able to achieve a modest standard of living and carve out a reasonable period of retirement with financial security.

Fast forward to today. Today, no such value has been put on retirement. We go along thinking, *There is nothing we can do, so why get upset?* Yet, there is everything we can do to prevent such a circumstance from happening to us. We just need to try.

Have you ever heard the expression "Luck is the residue of hard work"? It's true. Most people are "lucky" only because they worked hard at achieving a goal and through that hard work found success. So, first, be prepared to work hard at creating your own financial security. I promise you, it will not come easy, but with hard work, commitment, and focus, you will be on your way to solving your present financial challenges as well as preventing future financial challenges from becoming problems that prevent you from your deserved retirement.

The first step in facing our financial challenges is to accept responsibility of our present financial situation. In other words, whatever financial shape you are in right now, it is your fault, and your fault alone. Accordingly, it is up to you to fix any mess you might be in, without the benefit of others.

Credit cards

The biggest problems facing people today is the accumulation of consumer credit-driven debt. Lured by advertisements like "no interest for three years" or "don't pay 'till next year," we find ourselves purchasing items we have no business buying.

The secret to eliminating credit card debt is simple. Cut up your credit cards and throw them in the trash—now! Never again should anyone reading this book even think about a credit card. I have not used a credit card in more than ten years. That one practice has not only saved me thousands of dollars in wasted interest charges, but it has also freed from the worry that usually accompanies credit card debt. Peace of mind can be a priceless commodity.

My wife used to tell me I should have a credit card so I could build "credit." I told my wife then, as I say now, that the idea of "building credit" is hogwash! If I don't have the money to afford something, I should not buy it. Why do I need to "build credit"? That's like building a device that can blow up in our faces! We have been programmed to think we need credit. *I am here to tell you that the credit card companies need us; we don't need credit cards or the companies that come with them.*

The recent concept of the "credit score" is an interesting one. What is a "credit score," anyway? Did I take some kind of test that nobody told me about? Did you take some kind of test?

Nope. A credit score is based on a nonsensical mathematical equation that credit card companies use as a reason to overcharge you in interest rate fees. *It's time we all got together and gave the credit card companies a score of their own.* Personally, I'd give them a zero, because that's what I think they are worth. Credit cards serve only harm us financially. *Having a credit card gives us the opportunity to buy stuff we don't have the money for.* That should be reason enough to cut up those credit cards forever.

And then there are those "credit reports," issued by "credit reporting agencies" that never tell your side of your own credit history. The "credit reporting agencies" only tell the credit card's side of the story. Why is it that when you pay a bill early, your credit report does not report such an event? Ever try to correct one of those things? Good luck! Why would a "credit reporting agency" correct a report that they produce for the sole use of the credit card companies and banks? Forget it.

I think you can tell how I feel about credit cards, credit card companies, credit scores and credit reporting agencies.

I recommend you do without credit of any kind.

If you do without credit, you will not need to worry about a credit score, nor will you need to worry about a credit report. Take the power of your own financial life and put it back where it belongs—in your own hands.

Clearing your debt

Now that you have cut up those credit cards, you can begin to pay off those debts. If you have one job, consider getting a second job. Take your earnings from your second job and pay off those credit cards. Do not spend your earnings from your second job on anything but your credit card debt. As I said before, it is not easy. You need only to make up your mind to fix this challenge, and once you've obtained your second job, it will be only a matter of time before you are credit card–debt free. Stick with it, because it works.

Next, car loans. Time to bid *adios* to those too. Don't be upset if your neighbor is driving some fancy-schmancy car, because chances are, she doesn't own it! Most likely, that fancy-schmancy car is either leased or purchased with a ton of borrowed money. That means your neighbor is throwing away money every month for the privilege of looking good. My advice: Who cares what you look like driving a car that's paid off! In my book, you're looking pretty good financially, which is what you'll need to get to the financial promised land—*retirement*.

Now that you have realized you don't need car loans or credit cards, let us focus on the only debt that we actually do need to take out in our lifetimes—a home mortgage. Earlier I addressed mortgages, but only in respect to rising prices. I view a home mortgage as a necessary evil—not a good thing (because no debts are good) but necessary to obtain shelter.

My advice with respect to a mortgage is to treat a mortgage it like any other debt, which means the sooner you rid yourself of your mortgage debt, the better off you will be financially.

I would also like to caution you that a home should never be considered an investment for income purposes. A home is where you live, where you raise a family. A home may become an investment by accident, but *a home should be considered primarily where your heart is, not your balance sheet.*

Purchasing a home requires *discipline.* Don't be enticed into buying a huge residence if the purchase price is not in your range. I would recommend that you gauge how much you wish to pay for a home by multiplying your annual income by *no more than three times*, and then adding your down payment to that number. For example, if your annual income is $80,000 and you have saved $50,000 to buy a home, I would recommend you spend no more than $290,000 on a home. In this case, you would have to borrow $240,000 from the bank. I would recommend that you borrow, if possible, over a fifteen-year term to reduce your total interest costs over the life of your loan.

You should always take out a fixed-rate mortgage when choosing a mortgage product. Please do not get caught up in the allure of an adjustable-rate mortgage (ARM), as you may not be able to afford the payment when interest rates rise over time. Many banks like to sell you the idea that the mortgage is inexpensive, since many adjustable-rate mortgages offer initial interest rates below the market rate of interest. I caution you to beware of this type of mortgage, because many of these products generate much higher monthly payment obligations after the first two years of your loan. When the mortgage broker tells you not to worry because you can always refinance your mortgage, please remember: you may be falling into a trap. Depending on what the environment is for the real estate market when attempt to refinance, you may not have enough equity remaining in your home to qualify for a new mortgage. Accordingly, you will not be able to qualify to refinance your home, and thus you will be stuck paying a mortgage at absurdly high interest rates.

After living in your home for a few years, you should be earning more income. If that is the case, dedicate this extra income to paying an extra mortgage payment per year. Do not spend this extra money on anything else but your mortgage. You will thank me when you find that by making this extra mortgage payment each year, you will save thousands of dollars in interest charges.

Please don't listen to those folks who will tell you that you should not pay off your mortgage because you will pay more in taxes. That's a bunch of baloney! Sure, you might save some money in taxes, but you will lose two to three times those tax savings in wasted interest payments. Any way you look at it, you will spend more money by not paying off your mortgage. The sooner you pay off your mortgage, the sooner you can tackle the real challenge of your financial life—*your retirement.*

You may run across the theory that you should increase your contributions to our retirement plan instead of paying our mortgage. Again, my advice is that by paying down your mortgage debt, you are effectively increasing your retirement plan. First, you are saving the tremendous interest costs built in to your mortgage debt. Second, when you plan your retirement, chances are you will sell your home to generate cash to live on. The smaller the existing debt on your residence, the more net cash you will receive upon the sale of your residence, thus increasing the available funds for your retirement. Third, there is no guarantee that your retirement accounts will generate a rate of return equal to or greater than the mortgage debt you are paying off. You will likely receive less income from your retirement account if you put your financial gains in the hands of someone other than yourself. Trust yourself with your financial future. If you choose to trust an advisor, my advice would be "trust but verify."

The surest way to a solid financial future is, foremost, to eliminate your debts. This process can take a short time or a long time, depending on your present situation. If you have children, teach them now that building a life through debt is the wrong approach to financial success. Cut up your credit cards in front of your children to give them a dramatic example of how to take charge of their finances.

The best part of tackling your debt issues is that one day you will have succeeded. However long it takes, if you stay the course, you will succeed. I am aware that painful choices will have to be made, but if you sacrifice the temptation to spend money on non-essential items now, you will be in tremendous shape to conquer the main financial goal, which should be to fund your retirement.

Most of us have tackled the idea of losing weight or going on a diet. My approach to fixing your financial problems is similar. Think of it as a "financial diet." Our financial diet has all the similarities of a diet to lose weight. Think about it. What does it take to lose weight and keep it off? First, it takes a goal. Second, it takes the determination to avoid the temptations that contributed to our need to lose weight in the first place. It likely took many years of gaining weight before we realized we needed to lose weight and start our diet, and the same is likely the true with our debt issues.

Chances are we have utilized debt as a way of living for many years before realizing we've got to lose it. As with losing weight, it will take a commitment that spans months, if not years, to lose our debt, but most likely not even close to the length of time it took to gain our weight, or incur our debt. With each success, our debt gets thinner. With each success, we feel better and our mental outlook becomes more positive. We've just got to tighten our belts and cut the fat. It ain't easy, but once you become committed to this goal, you will be rewarded incrementally with every passing day.

The key to a successful diet is to fundamentally change the foods we eat and to maintain our bodies. The key to a successful financial diet is to fundamentally change the way we approach our finances and to maintain our financial discipline every day. We cannot live in our past mistakes, but we can live for our future successes.

What's next?

You've lost your financial weight, or debt. Now what? Well, you should have extra bucks lying around, unspent, at the end of each month. Now you will want to create an *emergency fund* for yourself. Every once in a while, the car will need to be repaired, the roof will start to leak, or the plumbing will break. (We all know how much a plumber costs!) Therefore, you will want to save at least two months' salary in a savings account for your emergency fund. Creating and maintaining an emergency fund will protect you against having to go back to those credit cards. Remember, never look back on those days. You need to create an environment that will enable you to avoid plunging back into the debt abyss.

Once you have established an emergency fund, you can get to the meat of your debt—your mortgage. The mortgage was designed to be a lifetime of debt. How cool would it be to disappoint those bankers by paying off a lifetime of debt in half the time! Paying off your debt in half the time would allow you to begin enjoying your life! What a concept! It's a shame that it never occurs to most of us.

Using the discipline you fostered in eliminating your credit card debt and establishing an emergency fund, you can now put the same contributions that went into establishing your emergency fund directly towards paying your mortgage.

Let us use our previous example of owning a home with a $240,000 mortgage. Let's also assume a 6 percent interest rate. That would make your monthly mortgage loan payment $1,438 on a thirty-year conventional mortgage. *Do you know how you can pay off your thirty-year mortgage in just 8.5 years?* A little more than double your mortgage payment, or a mortgage payment of $3009 per month, will pay off your debt in just 8.5 years!

I know what you're saying. "Yeah, that's great, but who the heck has an extra $1570 lying around each month to throw at a mortgage payment"? My answer is, you do!

Here's why.

Remember, in order to get to this stage of your financial diet, you have eliminated your monthly credit card debt and your monthly car payments. Think about it. Most folks are paying the credit card companies at least $1,000 a month, while most couples have two car payments, each payment about $300. That's $1,600 right there! You can do this—it just takes determination and time.

Let's say it takes you five years to eliminate credit cards and car payments and to establish an emergency fund. That's a lot of time, but let's say that's your worst-case scenario. Then, it takes 8.5 years to pay off your thirty-year mortgage. If you start this process when you are twenty-eight years old, at age forty-one you will be completely debt free. Now comes the fun part. Let's get to *retirement*.

Remember, as you get older, you earn more. If you stay on the financial path that you started 13.5 years ago, your earnings should theoretically free up more money each month for you to save. Let's assume you can save an additional $1500 per month after 13.5 years of belt-tightening. That means at age 41.5, you will be able to save the approximately $3009 you paid down your mortgage, as well as an additional $1500. That brings your monthly savings to $4,509. Let's use a compounded annual savings interest rate of 5 percent, net of income taxes. Saving $4509 each month at a 5 percent compounded rate of interest yields you, in just 13.5 years, an astounding $1,039,598. This brings you to age fifty-five. If you wish to work until age sixty-two, you would have saved for 20.5 years, which means your savings would total $1,926,316.

Now let's add the value of your home, which you purchased at, say, age twenty-eight for $290,000. We can safely assume the initial investment will have tripled by age fifty-five, and in theory quadrupled by age sixty-two. Don't forget the $500,000 you should have accumulated in your 401(k) plan at work by age fifty-five, or $800,000 at sixty-two. If I add up these assets, at age fifty-five you should have accumulated a net worth of $2,409,598, and at age sixty-two your accumulated net worth should be about $3,886,316. If we look at these values in the form of a monthly pension, at age fifty-five your monthly pension (assuming a 5 percent rate of return) should be $10,039. At age sixty-two, your monthly pension should be $16,192, without social security!

You owe every ounce of your success in funding your retirement to one person—yourself, because you were the one who took responsibility for your retirement by saving instead of spending.

Alternatives

After reading this stuff, you might be thinking, "Wow, a lifetime of discipline to retire? How come so and so made big bucks doing such and such and can retire today?"

Well, my direction as to how to get ahead in today's financial climate is rooted in *conservatism*. Nothing above involves the possibility of failure due to risk of investment. My financial plan is typically guaranteed by the *full faith and credit of the United States Government*, through insuring banking products that yield the required rate of return that you must purchase in order to meet the above stated financial goals.

Work and discipline for such a long time might not be for you. You might wish to invest in something other than guaranteed banking products to reach your financial goals. No problem. But please, if you choose this direction, heed the Latin expression *caveat emptor*, buyer beware.

My personal view of investing centers on *cycles of profitable economic sectors*. In simpler terms, "buy low and sell high." Sounds easy, but it becomes difficult when we get caught up in the "herd mentality" of investing our hard-earned savings.

You and I both know how difficult it is to save money in the first place, so I request that you look upon your savings account as "sacred," in the sense that your savings represent the sweat of your hard work and discipline. Approaching your savings in this manner may help you avoid the temptation of investing in a "get rich quick" scenario, such as a stock tip or a piece of real estate. My goal is to advise you to think long and hard before you choose an alternative investment that is not guaranteed.

CHAPTER 9

▼

WHAT YOU NEED TO
KNOW ABOUT THE
STOCK MARKET

The stock market, once considered extremely risky, is now perceived as part of our daily investment lives. There are a couple of reasons for this. First, as time passes, we are further and further removed from the stock market crash of 1929. Many see this crash as the fundamental reason for our economic suffering during the Great Depression. As a people, we lived in absolute poverty. Aided by the economic boom of the 1940s, due to World War II, as well as government legislation and regulation, we as a generation pulled ourselves out of poverty and into a period of relative prosperity.

I caution you that with each new piece of legislation that lifts the regulations instituted for our protection during the Great Depression, we risk coming closer and closer to the brink of another depression. Previously, our financial institutions were unable to own other businesses not involved with banking. Today, such legislation has been lifted, meaning the banking industry, and our savings dollars that support this industry, is exposed to risks associated with non-banking businesses. If we as a society place our economy in the hands of our banking system, then a large failure of that system could lead to an economic collapse on the scale of the Great Depression.

Another example of eliminating the safety nets implemented after the stock market crash of 1929 was the removal of the "uptick rule" in June 2007. The uptick rule was implemented as a safety measure to ensure that when stocks decline, a more orderly and accessible market would be available for the investor's exit from ownership of a given stock. The uptick rule enabled investors to limit their losses when stocks declined, as well as put obstacles in the way of a total collapse of the stock market. With the elimination of the uptick rule, the threat of a total collapse in the stock market is far more real. With banking institutions invested heavily in the stock market, the threat of a stock market crash triggering a collapse in the banking industry has increased exponentially.

Let me begin my discussion of the stock market with the basic concept of *supply and demand*. You are likely familiar with this concept, but let me go through it again to form the basis for my opinion of stock market investing.

Supply and demand of anything we own should dictate the price we pay for this ownership. If there is a large supply of anything we own and the demand for this ownership has remained the same, theoretically, the price of this ownership should go lower. Think of housing as an example. If the number of people wanting to buy a house has not changed, but a bunch of new houses have just been built and are up for sale, the price of these new houses should go down, because the sellers of each home would be competing against each other to entice you to buy their new home. Conversely, if the supply of new homes remained constant, but the demand (or the number of people wanting to buy new homes) increased, then theoretically the price for that new home should increase, because there would be more homebuyers than sellers. Basically, restrict the supply of anything and you increase the price. Increase the supply of anything, and you decrease the price. This of course, assumes that demand remains constant. Increase the demand of anything, and you increase the price. Decrease the demand of anything, and you decrease the price. Again, this assumes that the supply remains constant

What does this have to do with the stock market? Let me explain.

There is great risk inherent in the stock market that, amazingly, most folks do not know about, because no one has explained it to them. The fundamental risk of owning a stock of a publicly traded corporation is rarely fully explained to the average investor, because if people knew exactly what the risks were, they might decide not to invest in the stock market at all. Please note, I am not advising you to stay away from the stock market; I am simply advising you of the risks associated with the stock market that so few seem to be aware of.

Let me start by giving you some background. My work life involves dealing with the financial world on a peripheral level. I watch stock market fluctuations on a daily basis and have intently followed the fluctuations of the stock market very closely for twelve years. I was once an enthusiastic investor, hoping to build a retirement through ownership of stocks. I was aware that the stock market could go down in value but not why or how this happens. This is the most important issue relating to the stock market, as I came to understand fundamentally when my own personal portfolio decreased dramatically in value.

Investing in the stock market is a lot like gambling in Las Vegas casinos, in that the "house" or in the case of the stock market, the big money players that run the market, have to pay winners in order to entice you to gamble. If you knew the odds of winning in the stock market, you would most likely think twice before investing.

Why is the stock market so risky?

In late 2000, the value of my portfolio dropped seemingly every day. According to my financial advisor, this began when the Federal Reserve chairman decided to raise interest rates. According to my broker, my stock portfolio was decreasing in value because higher interest rates would slow the economy—the companies that I owned stock in would make less, thus the value of the companies (which supposedly traded their value based on earnings) would not earn as much profit, thus the companies would be worth less. At first, that explanation made sense, and I figured things would eventually turn around and stock prices would return to the level they were at before interest rates were hiked.

To my surprise, my portfolio continued to go down in value, even though there were no more interest rate increases to explain such a decrease. The next explanation, according to my financial advisor, was that the election of the President of the United States was in dispute, causing uncertainly, which nobody on Wall Street apparently likes. So my investments continued their decline in value. When we figured out who our next President was, I supposed that my portfolio would go back to its pre-election level. Guess what? My portfolio did not go back to its previous value; in fact, my portfolio continued to decrease in value!

Now, I was confused. A few months later, after the resolution of the election, a new reason for the continued decline of the value of my portfolio became apparent: *visibility*. Ahhh. Visibility. Wait, what did that have to do with the value of my stock portfolio? Well, according to my financial advisor, the CEOs of many companies had publicly stated that they could not predict with a certainty the future earnings of their companies, because their "visibility" was impaired due to a slowing economy. This so-called visibility impairment created uncertainty, and thus my portfolio continued its tortuous decline in value.

In fact, the Nasdaq stock market indicated a value of over 5,000 points in 1999. In late 2001, the point value of the Nasdaq stock market dropped below 1,400. This meant that the value of the companies listed on the Nasdaq stock market had decreased more than 72 percent in a little over two years.

How does anything go down 72 percent in value in so short a period? I never realized the real risk involved in investing in the stock market. I got to thinking: Since pretty much every person I know that invests in the stock market follows the philosophy of "buy and hold," this means they are not selling their stocks. I, of course, was not selling my stocks either. Now, let's go back to the idea of supply and demand. If my friends and I are not selling our stocks—and in fact, most people do not actively trade or sell their stocks—why does the value of stocks continue to decline? That means only 20 percent of stock owners actively sell. This severely tested my understanding of the basic principle of supply and demand. Once the 20 percent of stockowners sold, the stock prices should have stopped declining. Except that they did not stop declining. That meant that, somehow, people who did not actually own stocks were able to continue selling stocks, thus causing the price of stocks to decline.

How could this be? It made no sense. Think about it. What would happen to the price of houses in your neighborhood if a person could sell every house on every street in your neighborhood? Imagine a "for sale" sign on every house in your neighborhood. If every house on every street in your neighborhood went up for sale at the same time, don't you think that the flood of housing (supply) on the real estate market would cause a corresponding decline in the prices of houses, assuming the demand for houses remained the same? Of course housing prices would drop. But, you say, that cannot happen, because nobody is permitted to sell my home. Only I can sell my home. Should this same principle apply to the stocks I own? My answer is it should, but unfortunately it does not. In other words, *people who do not own stocks can actually sell your stock, the very stock you own.* This process is known on Wall Street as *short selling stock.*

Perhaps you've heard the term but never really thought about it. Here's how it works: you open up an account with a brokerage firm (for example, Morgan Stanley) and you ask your financial advisor to purchase 10,000 shares of stock in company X. Now you've essentially traded cash for 10,000 shares of stock in company X. You own these shares of stock, but they are sitting in your account at the brokerage firm. Many millions of people own of shares of stock in various companies that are sitting in their accounts at their brokerage firms. Now, what happens to money you deposit into your savings account at the bank? The bank actually uses your funds, lending it out to customers for loans. Similarly, *the brokerage house lends out your stock to daily stock traders.* Stock traders borrow your stock and in turn sell your stock on the open market. The stock trader, at an undermined future date, is required to return the borrowed stock. So, what happens when stock traders decide to short sell stock on the open market collectively? Stock traders will sell your stock, my stock, and anyone else's stock that brokerage firms make available to them. When our stocks are sold, repeatedly, with no change in the demand for our stock, *the value of our stock must decline.*

Eventually, after our stocks are sold many times over, the prices will collapse to a fraction of their original price. When the prices of our stocks fall to this level, the stock trader then purchases our stock on the market and returns the stock to the brokerage firm. The transaction is now complete—effectively the trader sold high and bought low, and we as owners of this very stock, sold without our consent, are left "holding the bag," in the form of a dramatically devalued portfolio.

The dramatic decline in stock values did not result in money just disappearing; on the contrary, the value of our stocks was transferred to the stock traders on Wall Street, while most of us knew nothing of this risk!

Reducing the value of our 401(K) plans by allowing people who don't actually own stock to sell them is a clever way of keeping the value of our pensions down, while the rich folks on Wall Street effectively take our retirement dollars. If you were aware of this risk—that the supply of a stock can be artificially manipulated to cause its value to drop—would you think twice before buying a stock? I know I now think twice.

This does not mean that investing in the stock market is a bad thing. You can make money in the stock market, but you should know the risks before you invest your hard-earned dollars. Remember, buying low and selling high is a good thing. So if you wish to buy a stock at a low price (chances are because the short sellers have manipulated the price of that stock), you should actually thank the short seller for getting you a bargain. Just don't buy into the hype of buying high. Chances are you will lose money.

Listen to your instincts

I seem to hear the same thing from financial folks when a stock is priced low: "They are going out of business." I remember in 1999 asking my financial advisor about the possibility of buying $5,000 worth of stock in a company called Western Digital. At the time, the stock was trading around $1.50 per share. The answer I received was, "They are going out of business. Terrible management." OK, I thought, don't buy their stock. Recently, that same stock traded over $20. If I had gone with my gut instinct, that $5,000 would now be $67,000. Not bad for a company going out of business. Then there is Xerox. Xerox traded down to $4 in 2000. My financial advisor said not to buy. Xerox was going out of business. "Bad financials." I bought a small amount, but not what my instinct told me to buy. Xerox rose from $4 to over $15. *Talked out of it again.*

I have been following a company for over two years now, Ford Motor Company. Just last week, another financial guy told me that if Ford does not merge with another company, they "are going out of business." Another trader had told me the same thing two months prior, when the stock price of this company went down to $6.50. In two months, the price of this particular stock has risen to $8.50, a 30 percent increase, and now it trading back down at $6.80. My financial guy still thinks it's a bad investment. I don't think so, but who am I to question such judgment? Just because this particular company has been in business for a hundred or so years, as well as having billions of dollars worth of assets, what do I know? I know enough to say that a few bucks (let's say 3 percent of your available investment capital) should be invested in such stocks. In this case, in the remote possibility that my financial guy is right and the company goes out of business, you've lost 3 percent of your investment capital. If my instincts are right, and the company stays in business, you will most likely double or even triple your investment over a few years' time.

Don't try to "catch a falling knife"

Never, ever, buy a stock on its way down. Following a chart of a company's stock price can be very helpful in this regard. Using the Ford Motor Company as an example, the company's charted stock price seemed to be on the downside, with no end in sight. So, I just waited until the bottom of the hill came into view on the chart. The stock chart performance indicated that over a twenty-year period, the company "bounced" off its low point (around $6.00) a few times. My instinct tells me that my risk of loss is relatively small if I decide to invest at about this point in the stock price. However, I want to wait until the price of this stock rebounds off this target. By viewing a charted history of a company's stock price, you can actually see when the downward spiral of a company's stock price hits its floor, and generally the price of a company's stock price rises from its floor only to fall back a second time. This is the point at which, if I am interested in investing in a particular company, I pay close attention to its chart performance. After the second rebound, I watch for the next rise in price. Should the price begin to move upwards and, while vacillating up and down, not fall to the floor again, I would now look to put my investment capital into this particular stock. I am no doubt taking a gamble, but I believe I have measured my risk and that it is limited.

If the stock price fell 30 percent below the historic charted low, I would sell, accept my loss, and move on. If the company stock price fell to such a point, the price could continue to spiral downward without a safe floor to depend on. This scenario is possible, but if you spread your risk over many different stock purchases, you will likely be successful more times than you fail. Think of it as making an educated guess.

Use stock charts

A popular method of identifying rising stocks is using a stock chart of a company to follow the price action as the price fluctuates in a narrow channel. The idea is that when the stock price goes above this narrow channel, it is ready to rise steadily and significantly. The theory holds that the longer a stock price trades within a range, or channel, the higher it should rise once it (the stock price) rises above the ceiling in the channel. I believe this is another excellent way to profit from picking stocks. Today, a perfect example is the stock chart of Time Warner (TWX). This company's stock price has been trading in the range of $15 to $19 per share for approximately five years. Recently, the stock price has moved to over $20. This price move has broken the "ceiling" of $19, and as such, I believe, is poised to move much higher. I would not be surprised to see the price of this particular stock rise 50 percent in a twenty-four-month period.

Using the tool of a stock chart when deciding to invest in the stock market is sort of like looking at a psychological profile of the herd of traders that brought down the price of a stock in the first place. Not only is this a fascinating science, but it is an approach that works more times than it does not.

More stock stuff

Stock prices rise and fall in cycles. For instance, for the past couple of years, the price of stocks in the area of pharmaceuticals (drug companies) have largely either fallen or traded within a very small range. Most of the companies in this area are well off of their high prices but have not made any real movement upwards in several years. This is an example of a cycle in which stock traders are moving another sector of the stock market up and getting ready to move into this particular sector when the traders decide to move out of the current sector of high performing stocks. As of 2005, real estate stocks have done well but have stopped rising. After watching the performance of the stock market for many years, my instinct tells me that the real money is quietly moving out of real estate stocks and into pharmaceutical stocks. When the big money has finally moved "all-in" to pharmaceutical stocks, you will see this sector of the stock market rise. The moral of the story is to monitor sectors of the stock market in three categories:

1. Sectors that are getting hammered (short sellers' delight)

2. Sectors that are quiet (big money's new home)

3. Sectors that are rising (big money's profits)

It's a wonderful thing to see where you should be at all times. You can do this by following the stock charts of companies in each sector. When you follow this path, you know where you want to be today and where you will be tomorrow. Just follow the money.

When do I sell a stock?

My opinion of when to sell is very simple. If you follow the chart performance of a stock, you can tell when it is about to get crushed by the short sellers. When a stock chart looks like a vertical line straight up, it's time to get out. This area of the stock chart is called "distribution," which is usually the time when the big money is hyping a stock to entice you to buy, while the big money is taking your money and moving into the quiet stocks. Usually, this is when some sort of "bad news" gets circulated around the stock market, and the short sellers come in and sell the tar out of the stock—just when the average retail investor is advised to purchase by financial advisors on those cable TV financial channels!

If you follow the charted price of a stock over time, you can see the relative top in its price. You will see the top only after the fact—the top is usually indicated by a break in a 45-degree upward trend line. Once the trend line of a stock falls below this 45-degree angle, chances are the stock is beginning its precipitous descent. If you did not sell your stock at vertical, get out now. Move into the quiet stocks and count your money.

Above all else, always be grateful when you sell at a profit—regardless of the size of the profit. The stock market is designed to take your money. When you make a profit, you essentially beat the stock market at its own game. And please, never, ever, get emotionally attached to a particular stock. When emotions enter the picture, objective, sound reason usually exits. If you've made money, sell and move on to the next parade. Eventually, the stock you've just sold will get crushed by short sellers. *My instinct tells me that we could see a sharp decline or just plain stagnation in the value of the stock market overall in a few years' time.* This is because the baby boom generation is nearing retirement age. If my thesis is correct, and most baby boomers will not have the means to retire, then the 401(k) plan of the baby boomer is also at risk. It cannot sustain real value. If the stock market increased in value on a large scale, then baby boomers would have the means, through their 401(k) plans, to retire, which we know is not what the rich folks want. Moreover, when the baby boomers begin to draw out their money from their 401(k) plans, as opposed to funding their 401(k) plans, then more actual dollars will be leaving the stock market rather than entering the stock market in the form of investment dollars. *When this happens, keep your money as far away from the stock market as possible,* because the market will have no other place to go but down.

Chapter 10

▼

Alternative Investments

Real estate

Usually, when one form of investment is going badly, an alternative form of investment will be going well. For instance, when the stock market was taking away our 401(k) money from 2000 to 2005, the real estate market went up tremendously. Of course, as I described earlier, this market was manipulated upwards to such high levels due to the manipulation of interest rates. Investing in real estate is a challenging option, but again, I caution you to buy low. Real estate, similar to any other asset class, goes through periodic cycles. Real estate prices can be manipulated up or down, as I explained earlier, by the raising and lowering interest rates. Interestingly, the supply of land cannot be manipulated, only the demand (because God stopped making land a long time ago). Herein lies the hidden safety of real estate investment. Eventually, your land values should increase as land becomes more scarce. However, this does not mean real estate is without risks. If you buy a piece of real estate at the high end of a rise in prices, and interest rates increase, the price of your investment will likely decline. In fact, you may not see your investment return to its original value for many, many years. So, again, you will want to follow the same philosophy of buying low and selling high. Please pay no mind to those folks that say you cannot "time" the market. When you hear this phrase, chances are, it is because you are being asked to purchase an investment when it is relatively high.

Small business

If you don't like to invest in the stock market and don't care to speculate in real estate, you can always try to *start your own business*. I must warn you, however, that 95 percent of business startups fail. Owning your own business can be financially rewarding, but it requires a commitment of both money and time. If you are self-employed, chances are you have very little time available for your personal life, because getting your business off the ground requires an enormous commitment of time.

The main reason for the failure of small business is lack of funding. Think of your business as the engine of your car. You will need to fund your business just as you need to put gasoline in your car to keep it running. Often small business owners need to take out the profits of the business to cover living expenses before the business is fully off the ground. Like a car engine without gas, the business stops working.

My advice for anyone looking to start one's own business is to be prepared not to take any salary from your business for the first five years of its existence. I know this sounds crazy, but if you are able to reinvest your profits into growing your business, it will grow to the point where you can draw a paycheck and not have a material effect on the bottom-line profits. Using profits for growth instead of personal consumption is the key to a successful enterprise, as well as the key to keeping your tax burdens low. Self-employment can be a very rewarding experience, and if run properly your business can even make you rich. You will likely need to take on more responsibility and commitment than you have ever accepted in any other endeavor. With commitment, discipline, dedication, and integrity, you can find success.

Closing Thoughts

I've attempted to address certain aspects of financial security that affect us all. By showing you the possibilities of
individual investment areas and warning you to pay attention to supply and demand, short-sellers, and timely
investing in all areas, I believe you can generate revenue in
multiple classifications of investments. Since we, as a
group, must individually generate our own profits (instead
of relying on the mega-corporation to fund our retirement), it's time to name our generation the "Revenue
Generation." It is a play on words, one that reflects the
notion that in order to be successful, we all need to adopt a
philosophy of generating revenue and minding our financial houses in a manner not too different from that of the
mega-corporation. We will have to make difficult decisions to cut the fat out of our personal lives, live more effi-

ciently, and build a sound foundation for our individual balance sheets to grow.

We also must be aware that as things constantly change around us, we have the power to correct mistakes that have put us on this path. Earlier I addressed the idea that the politician will be our downfall. This does not have to happen. We, collectively, can hold our politicians accountable for past legislation and future plans to correct such legislation.

If we dedicate ourselves to such a purpose, we can organize into one voice. For instance, if our local representative from Congress allows the mega-corporation to continue to strip away our retirements, we can collectively say "your fired!" by electing a representative that will change things. This process begins with each of us and grows with every neighbor we can gather to support our cause. The power of our collective voice can provide the instrument of change, but it must start with you and me. Remember, these economic issues affect not only our lives but also those of our children and their children. Getting involved in grass-roots efforts to begin the process of change works. But this requires a spirit of persistence, determination, and hard work. Sound familiar?

Looking back on the substance of my thoughts, I have articulated the mysteries of why we are not supposed to "get ahead," what you should do to make things right in your world of finance, what pitfalls await unsuspecting investors, and how you can make a success out of just about any situation. All is not lost. In fact, *opportunities for you to get ahead are everywhere*; you just need to know where to look and what to avoid. The bottom line is you need hard work, effort, dedication, commitment, discipline, and integrity to succeed financially. We all possess these qualities. Achieving financial success will not come easy, but with a fresh perspective, a plan, and a desire to meet your financial goals, you'll be on your way to a prosperous retirement. Why not start today?

"Opportunity is nowhere. You decide."

—Anonymous

Index

Note: Page entries followed by an "*f*" and "*t*" indicate that the reference is to a figure or table, respectively.

978-0-595-42069-8
0-595-42069-9

www.ingramcontent.com/pod-product-compliance
Lightning Source LLC
Chambersburg PA
CBHW030816180526
45163CB00003B/1300